PREFACE

I would like to take this time out to thank my friend, Ernest Newton.

Ernest inspired me to go on this trek to bring forth to the male gender this experience.

Yes, I said… "EPERIENCE"!

This is not a book!

Anyway!

My friend Ernest planted a seed of phenomenal proportions, deep within the reels of my psyche.   Something resonated…marinated…simmered and I was elevated! It was amazing…it seemed as if his story unlocked a door…a door deep within my consciously unconscious layer of effort, forth, hearth and, shall I say reign.

Yes, reign…I felt a   majestic awaking…a truth…an aired out freedom!

The caged bird as free!

THE CAGED BIRD WAS FREE!!!

Whatever did he say, you ask?

Now, what can a man say to another man to "wake up" something in him?

THE TRUTH!

The truth is simple, not hard...and so is life! Life is not hard! Life is, LIFE!

Now I'm going to give you guys most of the story as is, I know you'll get it!

Here we go!

So...a couple of days after Thanksgiving,g I called a great friend of mine, and I say great, for he may as well be blood.

Ernest, and my friend are brothers, so WE, are brothers.(AUSTIN NEWTON)

As we indulged each other in holiday salutations, we enjoys several chuckles of glee.

Honestly, we had a great communication, and Ernest grabbed the phone, and greeted me with love, as he always does.

As a matter of fact, lemme give you a couple facts about Big E! (That's his new nickname...formally E.L. Delquae)

But...

Ernest has the most welcoming home I've seen since...North Carolina!

He's hospitable, easy, genuine, honest,truthful, and his children...his children, you can tell, he's a great dad and influence.

The air in his home..is home...you can tell that you are in a...a....KING'S CASLTE!

You feel free and privileged to eat, drink and be merry!

I always enjoy the atmosphere, the good times and the goodness! The family comradery is second to none.

Now, E...new nick name...is a big man, and I was amazed at how much he smiled and was genuinely...for a lack of a better word...jolly!

Ernest, is a gentle giant...a calmed lion...a...a...foregoing hurricane with blistering winds...with a beautiful soul, filled with love and compassion and...and...and...

So....

As I listened to his parable, sprockets and clogs and transmitters got to moving and sparking...and I didn't know what was going on!

I thought I was high...maybe still hungover from the holiday partying...needless to say...SOMETHING WAS GOING DOWN IN MY HEAD!

The story was how he'd planned and prepared a great Thanksgiving holiday dinner.

While always intimate, enough is commonly cooked for family and visitors. As customary, Ernest always put forth his best effort in his food as he loves compliments and empty plates.

So, after deep frying a turkey, and accompanying it with all the fixings, Ernest, satisfied with himself wanted to relax...but yet he was informed, that the food he'd cooked was not going to be eaten...well...it was to be eaten but...not in his home!

As sugarplums danced in my head, cause E can burn...I was...mystified, confused and taken aback.

As he told his tale, I grew…"something"…I…I…felt some type of way!

But…but…he didn't stop, and as he told the story…he NEVER got UPSET!

Since he had no food to eat, Ernest decided to go visiting family, ended up at his brother's house(Austin), and everyone had a glorious time.

Funny thing though, E said, "When I woke the next day…" he was kind of chuckling.

"When I went to the refrigerator to get something to eat…everything I cooked was in there…they had too much food!"

Simple story, RIGHT?

Well I put myself in other people's temperament and I don't think anyone would be taking food out MY HOUES that I COOKED!

And the gargantuan question in my head was…

"How in the hell did you not end up in jail?"

Once I asked the question to him...more to myself...the doors with the answers opened in my subconscious...

"KING MODE"

So, as I explored this new door, I asked Ernest, "How'd you do it?"

He said, "What?"

I said, "Be able to stay in KING MODE like that? Something or a situation like that would drive me literally crazy and the whole Thanksgiving is a bust! How...how do you turn something that could definitively get in the creases and crevasses of any man...how do you make it into yet something petty? Because, by now, I know the party has a foolish inclination, for the actions taken were meant to hurt you...to belittle you! Amazing! Again, how do you do it?"

And, he said, "I don't know? I just don't like petty stuff, so I don't let it bother me!"

He gave me way more jewels as he spoke simple, plain, clear, clean English

and I soaked it up like a sponge...and so,
here we are!

THANK YOU ERNEST

A Seed

The truth.
It is what it is.
Or, it is what it is!
Or...it is what is?
From the minute, to colossal;
mind to tandem...
it is...
the light, of glow!

A.H. Faughsgate

A
King's
Mode

A H Faughsgate

Now, exactly…what is KING'S MODE? In short, I really can't describe or define it, but I will inform you, that I know it when I see it.

Another perfect example lies here in this next short tale.   You may be a little more familiar with this King.

George Foreman, at one time was held simply as the most ferocious fighter of all time.   His record was impeccable. His reputation was irrefutable and tenacity and will was unbreakable.

All of these traits and characteristics, makes great foundations for a King.

Now, George's story has to be shortened because his reign and story continues to unfold, even to this day, but we will focus on the highlights.

After totally abusing and man-handling Joe Frazier in the ring, Joe lost the title… to one known as the most feared boxer since Sonny Liston, George, was heralded as, "The Best!"

Even though, Ali dominated the sport from all angles, there was not a single inkling of skill, grit and rawness that could be ciphered from George.

So, as we look through history, we know that George bullied and obliterated the few fighters Muhammad Ali had troubles with, and even lost to.   He beat them sometimes, so effortlessly, it was a given and simply assumed, that he would do the same to, The Greatest!

The match, "THE RUMBLE IN THE JUNGLE"...was monumental!

The best and most feared against...The Greatest!

Two Kings...two kingdoms...both strong in their rights and in will and hearth!

A clash of titans!

WAR!!!

With simple plans and unfolding gumption...both men took upon their quests to execute their individual strategies.

Though, Muhammad Ali, created a new cutting-edge scientific counter approach to the stunning and stand-up straight power of George Foreman, and won the iconic fight...due to the amount of punishment imposed on Ali's body and head, it made it, a glamorous Pyrrhic victory.

All a while, the title... "THE GREATEST", was maintained and intact.

George, on the other hand seemed to fall deep into the shadows of his infamous lost!

But, that was only in the eye of, his subjects.   As a King George knew that your subjects will love you, then hate you, THEN, love you...AGAIN!

So never did George hold his head down in defeat...NO...you have never heard George complain about his lost...not one single time.

NOT ONCE!!!!

Mind you...he was Still a King!

Small kingdom or large!

In the inner-most sanctums of George's soul, he always understood the experiences of majestic endeavors.   He knew and comprehended the sacrifices that accompany such feats.   He fathomed the unseen.   He plotted, planned and maintained a regal air for himself... that was so solidified, when he decided to attempt a comeback...his boxing stature, bulleted him to a title match!

And....and, lo and behold...
A KING'S MODE
I cant describe it...but I know it when I see it!

One more quick yarn...one of a soul on the path, but not so Kingly, yet.   In search of, and knocking!

This one is of yours truly! Yes, me, I search for riches and endeavors of excellence, and too, I know all too well, the path!

I find myself in situations of lost self-control...(mostly personal)! Nonetheless. I fail to...to...be able to, conjure the self-discipline to exercise the... "not needed and degraded thoughts"!

So I admire people like Ernest and George, and, I wrote from back to front...so by now my mind is...yes, elevated and deviated from the deviance.

But, it took me this long, plus, a simple story by a man that could easily, for a lack of a better word...”Hulk Smash!”...some shit, so... I said...to myself, I’m not listening to his mouth anymore, I need to know what was his thoughts!

And E said, “Mane...” you know he from Atl, Georgia...

“Mane, I’ont be worrin’ bout dat petty stuff!”

THE WHOLE DINNER, AND THAT’S PETTY...LET’S GO KINGS!!!

The Experience laid here before you, is going to help you to develop, understand and harness the idea and power of your thoughts...

"A thought and a seed, is the same thing!"
A.H. Faughsgate

What is thought...a thought....thought?
Remember this equation, thought is equivalent to a seed, it seems small but...within its potential is very possibly, an Oak tree.
Thought is the seed to action, and thought and actions sum is situation.

```
    THOUGHT
    +ACTION
    -------------
    SITUATION
```

Make it hard if you want to! Remember life is simple, its not hard...its life! Keep it simple.

For example, Laws of the Universe, are simple...
The Law of Gravity
The Law of Attraction
The Law of Oneness

These Laws are simple, but absolute, so why would the entire universe be simple, and get complicated at "HUMAN"?

Do you know what a human is? You cant look it up in Webster.   Your understanding has to stay simple.

A human is a trifecta, a...perfect storm to even say the least, the perfect cosmic combination of Spirit, Soul and Body.   They all work in harmony simultaneously at all times...whether you are conscious of it or not.

The perfect conspiracy theory, for whenever one is removed...you no longer exists.

Who are you?

You are the sum of your thoughts! Your actions may say, and you mouth may say...but your thoughts are the truth and the truth is the truth...is the truth!

"I think, therefore...I am!"

"Mind is always superior over matter."
The $1,000,000 question is...
"Where are your thoughts?"
Thought, (seed)...has power.   A man is what he thinks.   He is an accumulation of his thoughts...
"...thoughts are wrought like iron..."
To be "KING", is no less...to be even considered a King, one is simply a culmination of a life long effort of fortitude and dedication.
In... "King Mode"...there is an understanding that, you make and destroy you!
Man, as in HUMAN, is the only mammal that can effectively control its thoughts.
Therefore if we keep our equation simple...good thoughts, yield good,

actions bringing forth, good situations and outcomes, and of course the equal is opposite.

No Comprhende'?

The mind is like a plant!

Thought or seed and the product or fruit it brings forth, is one.

You can only get melons from melons and you can only get fig from a fig tree.

So, the man is simply a circumstance of his thoughts.

'...harmony creates the ripest fruit..."

Being in harmony, is a tandem experience with the universe.

When you and the universe, sync with your thoughts, actions and situations...that's harmony!

When you have situations of ailment, disease or degradation...you and your thoughts and actions and situation are not aligned.

To make any major change in your life, you must begin with the way you think.

"... everything has a vibration that carries through the universe...even thought..."

Thoughts have vibrations! Even your innermost thoughts have a signal that is sent throughout the universe, and therefore, in the universe, there are no secrets.

Thoughts manifest themselves as habit, and habits in turn create situations.

Impure or immoral or corrupt thoughts, manifest themselves as confusing, untrustworthy and sneaky habits, that frustrates harmony which in turn creates situations of hardship and distraction!

Thoughts of fear manifest themselves in ways of having weak, unmanly, timid and unconfident habits.   Habits that in turn create situations of failure, aloofness, disdain and off-the-mark dependency.

Lapsy daisy or lazy thoughts congeal as habits of procrastination, dishonesty, mistrust and filth.   These habits create situations of vagrancy, degradation, emptiness and loneliness.

Envious, jealous and/or evil thoughts, become tangible in habits of contempt, deviousness, slyness, lies even violence.

These ugly habits, from thought...creates situations of hate, animosity and often danger!

Selfish thoughts, manifest themselves as habits known as, self-fulfilment tactics, that creates situations of contentment, high-stress and accusation.

Same coin, beautiful, great and wholesome thoughts manifest themselves in grace, openness, kindness, being trustworthy with the ability to create true and genuine situations to advance in every way.

Pure inclinations become tangible in contentment and control...creating life experiences with peace, wisdom and earnest.

Confident, Strong and assertive thought processes habitual actions that create life situations such being a leader, being successful, and… loving and/or selfless thoughts manifest themselves in characteristics such as true empathy, sympathy and genuine concern for others, leading to life situations such as being prosperous and having lasting and strong relationships.

"You will be what you will to be…"

The universe hears and complies with your innermost ambitions, wishes, wants and thoughts. A clean mind is the most powerful tool as well as a blank canvas.

Did you know that you can scare yourself to DEATH? FEAR!!!!

Thoughts of strength invigorate the body and soul, while thoughts of weakness and fear does the opposite.

Did you know that lying was bad for your health? Lying is believed to release stress hormones, that increases your heart rate.

Clean thoughts, clean heart, clean body…yields a clean mind to manifest themselves in a clean and healthy and strong life!

So now, we understand that thought is the seed of all of life's reap.   Thought ignites and is the catalyst for action, life and almost anything tangible.

Protect and guard your mind as you would your body.

"...cleanliness is next to Godliness..."

Ugly, dark and diminishing thoughts can create an abyss of lost purgatory that only leads to darkness, liken to a prison.

"...there are no bad experiences..."

Unselfishness is contagious as well.

If you want peace, give peace.   If you want love give love. The power is and always will be in your hand.

An aimless or wandering mind is the Devil's playground.

The strongest will survive!

The strongest, "will", will survive!

Think forward, strong progressive thoughts.   Your thoughts have purpose, and your purpose is driven by your thoughts...thought and purpose...cause and effect.

Thoughts are focused signals vibrating throughout the universe while daydreams and imagination are mere distractions.

Once your inclination is consciously received as a signal recognized on its vibratory wave, there nothing that can stop it.

If you have a weak mind remind yourself that the weak man makes himself strong by working out and taking particular care of his body, as so, you will do the same for your mind.   Strengthen your mind to control your thoughts to control the manifestations, to control the situations, to control your life.

Failure is only a pit-stop, a mere trip back to the drawing board.   Eliminate doubt and fears.   Shadowy unconfident thoughts have never accomplished anything...never have and never will.

Fear is the mortal enemy of a "Can Do", attitude.

Doubt is the father of hesitation, procrastination, devastation, deviation and ultimately your destination. Slay doubt and fear as if you were a fearless Roman warrior on the front line, fighting with all his might to represent for his king…knowing nothing can stop victory.

Pillage those weak thoughts of doubt, of all of its numbing and immobilizing powers.   Strengthen your psyche by purifying your thought process.

"…if you search…then you shall find…"

"Knock and the door will open!"

Self-control is strength.

Will power shows reserve!

Calmness is power!

Righteous thoughts empowers and blossoms into mastery!

Your thoughts create the individual "YOU".

We, as men, are so eager to improve our circumstances, but, yet…we are unwilling, even sometimes refuse to improve the self…therefore, most of the time, no accomplishments.   We must start within,   because our thoughts are the "foundation" of everything we intend to "build" for ourselves.   You must have a solid foundation! With a weak foundation, you can build nothing on it, but, with a strong solid foundation, you can build to the moon and back.

Control your emotions.   Our emotions, influences and basically dictates our thoughts and our thoughts manifest themselves, primarily, from how we feel.

The human being is one of the greatest feast in the universe, a perfect storm of included cosmic, celestial and spiritual entities...mixed in an aged-old recipe to create us!

Live with purpose and think with majestic inclinations to better thyself and others around you.

Be willing to accept the responsibility and consequences of thought.

You are the sum of what you inspire...as well...the difference, too.

As so far, for any man to be in KING MODE successfully, he must already be "KING" in his thoughts, impressions, manifestations, actions, habits and presence.

Understand sacrifice is always lurking, but, can be made effortlessly with forward thinking and strong habitual gratuities to the universe by way of traveling on a positive, enlightened and loving vibratory lane within the universe.

How to understand 12 of the laws of
the universe to harness their power
to improve your life.

1. Law of divine oneness

The law of divine oneness is the MVP of
the universal laws, in that it's the one
upon which all others build. "This law
states that we are all connected through
creation," Wilder says. "Every single
atom inside of you is connected in some
way, shape, or form to the rest of the
universe you move through."

This means that everything we do has a
ripple effect and impacts the
collective—not just ourselves. To call
upon this principle for self-improvement,
simply remember that your actions both
matter and make a difference.

2. Law of vibration

"Everything in the universe has a
frequency and a vibration," Wilder says.
"Nothing ever stands still, as everything
is always either being pushed away or

pulled toward something." Furthermore, items of a similar vibration are attracted to each other. So, to use this law to manifest your desires, you must match your vibration with that of what you want.

3. Law of correspondence

The premise behind the law of correspondence is that our lives are created by the subconscious patterns we repeat every single day, and these patterns either serve us or hold us back, Wilder says. Activate this law by becoming aware of your own patterns, which are often passed down via family ties, and then consciously taking action steps to break them.

4. Law of attraction

"This is the law of vibration in action," Wilder says. "Many people get scared by the notion that bad thoughts or low vibrations can somehow destroy their life because they're unaware. The law is not a punishment, but a very clear mirror of our

self-worth and mind-set. You're
surrounded by the outcome of decisions
you've made in the past and are fully
capable of making other decisions and
attracting a different set of
circumstances."

5. Law of inspired action

While the law of attraction is about
vibrationally aligning yourself with
whatever it is you want, the law of
inspired action is about taking—you
guessed it—action in order to bring what
you want to fruition. So you can certainly
create vision boards, but Wilder says
taking physical steps to move you closer
to your vision is much more crucial.

6. Law of perpetual transmutation of energy

"This law means that even the smallest
action can have a profound effect,"
Wilder says. "Like the seed of a mighty
tree holds all its promise in its tiny shell,
you also have the power within you to
move mountains."

To put the law into action on a practical level, Wilder recommends doing small things every day that uplift you, whether that's singing in the shower, dancing like nobody's watching, or anything else. Remember, small shifts equal major results.

7. Law of cause and effect

The law of cause and effect, also known as the law of karma, states that any action causes a reaction, Wilder says, and that whatever you put out—good or bad—you get right back. To harness the power of this law, be aware of how your actions and decisions are affecting not just yourself but everyone around you, and focus on sending out good vibes only.

8. Law of compensation

The law of compensation is about reaping what you sow. "It instills trust in us that we will be compensated for our work as long as we're open to receiving in all the many ways that the universe can deliver," Wilder says.

To be clear, compensation in this sense isn't limited to employment arrangements or financial compensation. Rather, it's about receiving compensation for all your contributions to the world around you, including the love, joy, and kindness you spread; it is all rewarded.

9. Law of relativity

"Nothing and no one is inherently good or bad," Wilder says. "Everything is a spectrum of expression, and there is more than one perspective on any situation or challenge." In other words, we are the ones who assign meaning to things, so we can choose to regard things as "bad" or as happening in our favor.

10. Law of polarity

Everything has a polar opposite: If there's an up, there's a down. If there's light, there's dark. One cannot exist without the other. Wilder says experiencing these polarities is part of the human experience, and that they also help us learn from our mistakes and support us in identifying

what we don't want so we can get clearer
on what we do want.

11. Law of perpetual motion

The law of perpetual motion tells us that
everything is forever changing and our
job is to embrace the ride. "If life is tough
and challenging, know that it will
change," Wilder says. "If everything is
peachy, then savor the moment, but don't
try to make it last beyond the natural
order of things. Each stage of life has
tremendous gifts to offer."

12. The law of giving and receiving

The energies of giving and receiving
operate within all of us, and in order to
create flow, they need to be in balance.
"To work with this law is to recognize
where in your life the balance between
giving and receiving is off," Wilder says.
"You have to allow both sides in you to
have their say and get their way."

Brought to you byhttps://www.wellandgood.com/laws-of
-the-universe/

100 words all Kings should know

1. Acquiesce This word means that a person has agreed or assented either verbally or tacitly to something. Even when it is well understood, this word is often misspelled.

2. Aberration Sometimes, it's good to be different, but the word "aberration" describes an unwelcome oddity. So, if someone accuses you of aberrant behavior, they aren't complimenting your originality.

3. Abjure If you solemnly renounce something, you have abjured it. The word is used in baptism ceremonies in certain churches. The person being baptized declares that he or she abjures Satan and all his works.

3. Abrogate Abrogation is a situation in which formal or legal measures are taken to do away with something. This would usually be a law or a formal rule that is repealed or temporarily suspended.

4. Acronym This should have been an easy one for lovers of language. An acronym is an abbreviation consisting of letters. For example, U.S.A for United States of America.

5. Anachronism I'm sure you will have encountered a few anachronisms during your life. An anachronism is something that is out of date and no longer relevant to the times. If you want to argue that something has lost its relevance by not changing with the times, you can describe it as being anachronistic or an anachronism.

6. Anathema No, it's not a rather nice sounding girl's name. It describes something that you vehemently dislike to the point of total rejection. For example: "He is an atheist; all forms of religion are anathema to him."

7. Antebellum A thing that is described as "antebellum" was conceived or constructed prior to an important war. The plantation era before the American Civil War is sometimes referred to as the

antebellum era, but the word can apply to anything that preceded a major war.

8. Anthropogenic Anything that has been caused by human interventions is anthropogenic. The word is usually used in the context of environmental degradation and pollution. Climate change, for example, could be described as an anthropogenic phenomenon.

9. Antithesis Something or someone that is the diametric opposite of something else. "He was the antithesis of the frivolous millionaire playboy," would imply that the person was the opposite of what one expect from a happy-go-lucky millionaire. Perhaps he was very serious about current issues, or didn't like wasting money on status symbols.

10. Assonance This is the sound a donkey makes. Alright, I'm kidding again, but it does have something to do with sound. It is a technique often used in creative writing and poetry in which similar sounding (but not necessarily rhyming) words are used in close proximity to one another.

11. Benchmarking Benchmarking involves selecting a certain state as being the norm against which other, similar things will be compared. For example, in vegetation surveys, undisturbed nature would be seen as the benchmark against which vegetation would be evaluated.

12. Bellicose This is a lovely word for describing people who are aggressive and even willing to fight over an issue. As you can imagine, bellicosity and politics often go hand in hand!

13. Bowdlerize This is a form of censorship that not only removes the portions of text some might consider risqué, but also weakens the work. The original Bowdler, published an expurgated version of Shakespeare. "Nothing is added to the original text; but those words and expressions omitted which cannot with propriety be read aloud in a family," he wrote, blithely unaware that his 1818 work would turn his name into a byword for literary slaughter.

14. Chicanery "Chicanery" alludes to the use of dirty tricks in the financial, political or legal world. If you are ever accused of it, know that you are in deep trouble!

15. Chthonic You really won't see this word in everyday use, but it's a killer if you're into word games! It refers to caves or the underworld. It is a synonym for the more well-known "subterranean" .

16. Cerulean You will no doubt have read about cerulean waters or skies and assumed that they were blue. You are right. Specifically, the word refers to a deep, sky-blue.

17. Circumspect If you are behaving with circumspection, you are watchful, wary or unwilling to take risks. One could almost say it was an antonym or opposite for "bellicose"!

18. Circumlocution Have you ever talked to someone who explains things in a roundabout way? They are guilty of circumlocution. They literally "talk

around" a subject instead of being specific and concise.

19. Cogent The person who is guilty of circumlocution, should try to be more cogent. In other words, they should be clear, logical and convincing. When you present arguments, you will strive for cogency.

20. Colloquial This is the kind of language we use every day. It is the "spoken" form of a language, and is not appropriate when you are writing a formal text. That doesn't mean that colloquial words are wrong or bad. They are simply informal.

21. Conundrum A conundrum could simply be a riddle, but it is also used to describe any puzzling or difficult question.

22. Crepuscular This lovely word is used to describe things that resemble or relate to twilight. In its simplest form, it is used to describe creatures that become active at twilight, but I'm sure you know a few people like that too!

23. Deleterious If something has harmful effects, they can be described as "deleterious effects." You'll often find this word being used in medical texts and in psychology. "Harmful" is just as good, but this word is ever so much weightier!

24. Depredation My mom used to use this word to describe my brother's activities in the pantry. It describes an act of attack or plunder. Judging from the state of the grocery cupboard once my brother was finished, my mom described what he'd been up to very well.

25. Didactic In its simplest context, this word describes something that was designed to teach a lesson. For example, a didactic story would have a strong lesson to teach. However, the word can also be used negatively to describe someone who is preachy and patronizing.

26. Egregious Think of all the words that mean "terribly bad or shocking;" that's what "egregious" means. Never did a difficult-seeming word have a simpler definition!

27. Enervate If you are feeling drained, weakened and tired out, you have probably been through some sort of enervating experience. There are good types of tiredness, but this is not one of them.

28. Enfranchise This means giving people freedom or the right to vote. Nowadays, we worry about disenfranchisement, a situation in which rights or freedoms are taken away.

29. Entomophagy This word is quite rarely used, but if we were to have a famine, or if certain exotic dishes became popular, we might need it. It means "the eating of insects," and although it generally applies to animals and birds, there are plenty of people who eat insects as a matter of course! Any word with the suffix "phagy" or "phagous" refers to what an organism eats.

30. Epiphany   An epiphany is an "Aha!" moment, but the word comes from the Christian festival celebrating the revelation of Christ to the magi. If you

have a life-changing realization, it could be described as an epiphany.

31. Epitome A perfect example of something epitomizes it. "Her life so far is the epitome of the American Dream," makes me think, "Wow, I want one just like it!"

32. Eschatology A lot of people discuss this quite heatedly without knowing the right word for it. It is a religious doctrine that deals with death, judgement, and what happens to the soul after death. And in case you were wondering – I didn't know this word before I researched this article, but I thought we needed a few challenges.

33. Eschew Here's a useful little word that says more than it seems to. For example, you could say someone doesn't exercise, but if you say, "He eschewed exercise," it implies a stronger and more deliberate aversion.

34. Evanescent If you have literary ambitions, this beautiful word is worth having in your vocabulary. It refers to

something that is transitory, or that disappears or fades rapidly.

35. Existential The word structure says it all. It describes something to do with the nature of existence. If you're into philosophy, you probably use this word a lot.

36. Exponential There is a mathematical description of exponents and what can be regarded as "exponential." I'm not going to go into it here. We more often hear of it in a context that implies rapidly increasing growth. When you hear it, don't just trust it. Ask for the figures.

37. Facetious This is one of my all-time favorite words, and I have frequently been accused of facetiousness. It means making inappropriate jokes or taking serious situations too lightly. I wouldn't say it's always a good thing, but sometimes, it helps, because there are times when we are way too serious about unimportant things.

38. Fascism What is it? It sounds great in political arguments, and the word is often

bandied about. It is a type of nationalism that sprang up in Europe in the 1920's, and it led to some pretty authoritarian governments that were known for their right-wing views and intolerance. If you want to know more about the deeper implications of fascism, read some history.

39. Fatuous A fatuous comment is silly, inane, or just plain stupid. Save this remark for someone who really deserves it, and serve it up cold.

40. Fiduciary If you encounter this word, it will be in a legal context. It is the term used to describe a trustee who takes care of assets on behalf of one or more beneficiaries.

41. Filibuster The filibuster is a person who uses a dirty, time-wasting trick to hold up a legislative decision. Without breaking any rules, the filibuster speaks at great length without saying anything useful. The word comes from the old English for "pirate," and it is not a good thing to be.

42. Fulminate Let's use an example: your teacher tells the class that the holiday assignment is a 10,000-word essay. After class, everyone discusses how furious they are, how unfair it is, and so on. They are, in fact, fulminating.

43. Hegemony Ever since people first got together to live in cities, there have been groups of citizens with differing cultural or social backgrounds. When one group politically dominates all the others, it is called a "hegemony," and the term can be applied to any form of government that fits the description.

44. Heuristic If someone once helped you to work something out for yourself, he or she used a heuristic teaching method. You could call it "hands on" learning, but nobody shows you what to do. They just show you how to figure it out, and you get to feel great when you get it right.

45. Holistic The simplest definition for this would be to say that holism considers various factors that influence each other, and not just one factor, influence or symptom in isolation. The term is most

commonly used in philosophy and medicine, but it is getting quite commercialized, and is sometimes used elsewhere too.

46. Homonym When two words are spelled the same, are pronounced the same, but have different meanings, they are homonyms. For instance, "The man standing beside the pole is a Pole."

47. Hubris In Greek mythology, hubris was a state in which mankind defied the gods or thought itself better than the gods. Dreadful consequences predictably followed. Today, it means excessive pride or confidence that could lead to terrible consequences.

48. IncisiveHave you ever tried to explain how you feel about something at length only for your listener to sum it all up in a sentence or two? That's incisive thinking. It gets to the heart of the matter quickly, showing great insight.

49. Incognito Are you mysterious? Then you may like being incognito – using

another identity or concealing your own identity in some other way.

50. Inculcate This means teaching someone a principle or habit in such a way that the lesson is fully ingrained and adopted.

51. Interpolate Interpolating something means inserting it between fixed points. The word is often used to indicate that something has been added to a book or text. Perhaps there are images, or perhaps a third party has added information. It can also be an interruption when someone is talking.

52. Irony Too easy? Nevertheless, this word is often incorrectly used. Irony means saying the opposite of what you mean for effect. Sometimes, events can be ironic for the same reason: they seem to contradict each other. Many people confuse it with sarcasm.

53. Juxtaposition When two contrasting situations or thoughts are compared for effect, we have a juxtaposition. It's a

useful technique in both creative and factual writing.

54. Jejune If someone presents you with a naïve point of view, seems to be oversimplifying, or has only superficial knowledge, you can use this word, both to describe their efforts, and to baffle them.

55. Lionize When you treat someone as if they were a celebrity, then you are lionizing them. Sometimes, we do this out of genuine respect for what they do, but sometimes, people do it to gain favor.

56. Lucubration The word "lucubration" could be used to indicate something that has been given a lot of study and deep thought, but it's also a rather rude way of describing a piece of writing that seems terribly pedantic and overelaborate.

57. Malapropism The word "malapropism" was coined thanks to a 1755 play by Richard Sheridan. Mrs. Malaprop would often replace words with similar sounding ones with amusing results. If you talk about having "danced

the flamingo" you are guilty of a malapropism.

58. Magnanimous When someone is very generous or forgiving to someone in a less powerful positon, you can call him or her "magnanimous." It's a form of generosity that isn't really necessary, but that shows kindness.

59. Mnemonic When you use a combination of letters, a rhyme, or a set of associated things to remember a list of names or facts, you are using mnemonics.

60. Motif A motif could be something as simple as a design on a Tee shirt, or it can be a theme in writing or music. A leitmotif is a "leading motif" that is one of several motifs, but is dominant. In music, it could be a theme tune associated with a particular character.

61. Moiety In anthropology, this term relates to the groups into which people are divided during important rituals, but it has also come to mean a share, particularly a lesser one.

62. Nihilism "Nothing matters, everything is trivial, even existence is questionable and could be an illusion. There is no God, and nothing has any importance." If this depressing philosophy appeals to you, you are a nihilist.

63. Nomenclature A nomenclature is a system designed for naming things. It could be a set of terminology, a term, or it could refer to a scientific naming system such as that used to identify all living things with two Latin names.

64. Nemesis You don't want to meet this person or circumstance. It is an "inescapable agent" that leads to your downfall.

65. Obfuscate Scenario: you have just been to class. Your teacher has explained something at length in terms that have left you totally confused. Scenario two: you ask a friend why they did something you don't quite approve of, and they give you a long story that leaves you feeling baffled. Words can be used to clarify, or they can be used to obfuscate facts.

66. Obsequious People are bowing and scraping and offering every possible tribute to someone in power. You have a feeling they're being obsequious because of the servile degree of attention they are giving.

67. Oligarchy A small group of people with very similar interests have absolute control over the destiny of a country or an institution. Does that sound scary? Now you know what to call it!

68. Onomatopoeia "Bang! Crash! Zoink. Kerflabaflabaflaba!" Words that are meant to imitate sounds are examples of onomatopoeia.

69. Ontology What is the metaphysical nature of being? Do you have an opinion? That's ontology! Don't even ask me about mine…

70. Orthography How are words spelled? That's orthography right there!

71. Oxymoron I'm sure you know a few phrases that are contradictions in terms. Some say that "military intelligence" is

one of them. Which oxymoron is your favorite?

72. Paradigm If you go into business, you will hear this word rather a lot. It means a model that governs the way things are done, and they'll usually be telling you that you need to shift it, or that there is a new one.

73. Paucity When there is too little of anything, you are suffering a paucity of it. It's most often used in relation to facts, but it works just as well and even more uncomfortably with funds.

74. Pecuniary How remarkable that this word should follow my last incisive remark! Pecuniary considerations are about money. Please do not use them as the sole basis for choosing a career. You will be unhappy, but will have achieved pecuniary gain.

75. Pedantic Sometimes, it's good to be fussy or finicky about the way you present information, but if you go too far with it, people will call you "pedantic."

76. Pedagogy Pedagogy is teaching, and a pedagogue is a teacher, but this old-fashioned word is often used negatively to describe someone who teaches rather boringly.

77. Pejorative If you're inclined to disapprove or disparage something, you are being pejorative. Pejorative words express disapproval.

78. Phonemes Phonemes are letters that distinguish very similar words from one another. For instance, "pad, pat, bad and bat" are distinguished from each other by phonemes.

79. Plagiarism As a student, you need to understand plagiarism and know how to avoid it. If you were to copy whole passages from someone else's work, that's plagiarism. Of course, plagiarism is something to be avoided whenever you are supposed to be producing original work.

80. Proletariat If you are an average working class person, you are a member of the proletariat. The word was

extensively used in Marxist philosophy, but now it's fair game for anyone to use.

81. Prolix When someone calls your written work "prolix," you should not congratulate yourself. It means you have presented it in an overly complicated, wordy, or rambling fashion. It's also a great scrabble word. Just imagine the score if you hit "triple word score" with it!

89. Pusillanimous Cowards, the lily-livered and the generally timid may be deserving of a suitably disparaging adjective. This is it.

80. Quotidian You could use this word to describe something that is mundane or that happens every day. If you're looking for a synonym, try "everyday" for size. In medicine, it is used to describe a particularly nasty form of malaria.

81. Reify Never let it be said that we only looked at long words. This one means turning something abstract into something more real and easier to understand.

82. Rubric There are three meanings for this word. It could be a statement of purpose or function, a simple heading at the top of a document, or a note in a liturgical book indicating how a ceremony should be performed.

83. Sanguine I like people with a sanguine disposition. They are upbeat and optimistic. You can, for example, be sanguine about the future, your economic prospects, and so on. Of course, that doesn't necessarily mean you are being realistic!

84. Scurrilous Being scurrilous could mean everything from being humorously insulting to being downright libelous and spreading nasty rumors.

85. Sesquipedalian What could be better than a really long word to describe the use of long words? I have to admit, this is one of my favorites, simply because it seems so appropriate, and rather funny.

86. Soliloquy Nowadays, if you were to talk to yourself about what your thoughts and feelings, people would think you had

gone mad. Nevertheless, the soliloquy has been widely used in drama to give audiences an insight into the character's thoughts.

87. Tautology There are two ways to use this word. A tautology could be an unnecessary repetition – repeating the same idea using different words. It could also be used to describe logic that is undeniably correct and proves a truth.

88. Temerity When you need a word to describe an action that is outrageously cheeky or audacious, this word is perfect for the job, "He had the temerity to decide I wouldn't mind him copying my work."

89. Ubiquitous Anything that is everywhere to be found or seems to be so is "ubiquitous." "Text speak is becoming so ubiquitous that it may soon be accepted in business letters."

90. Umami Your tongue can identify a number of flavors. Umami is a meaty flavor that is not sweet, sour, or salty.

91. Vernacular The language you speak at home, or the one spoken by a specific group of people in a country or region is its vernacular language. It also refers to architecture that focuses on what is functional.

92. Verisimilitude Is something real? Is it true? Are you unsure? Then you are doubting its verisimilitude. This word is handy because it combines the concepts of truth and reality.

93. Vitriolic When people are vitriolic, I either find it very funny (which they don't intend) or annoying. Vitriolic speech or writing is bitter, caustic and acerbic.

94. Ultracrepidarian Do you know someone who always has advice for you no matter how little knowledge he or she has? Now you have the right word to describe this person!

95. Unctuous It's usually very nice when people admire you, but sometimes you get the feeling that a person is being oily or insincere, and just wants to get into

your good books. When this happens, you have just been the object of unctuous behavior.

96. Uxorious When a man is overly submissive towards his wife, he can be described as "uxorious." Of course, she might just say that's just how it should be!

97. Vacuity "I admire your vacuity," he said. "Why, thank you," she replied, proving the point. Vacuity is empty-headedness and a lack of intelligence.

98. Xeric Generally, when we see the prefix "Xero" or "Xer" we can associate the word that it introduces with something very dry. A xeric life form can tolerate, and even prefers very dry conditions, and a xerophyte, is a plant that tolerates extremely dry environments.

99. Zymurgy This is a very helpful scrabble word, but what does it mean? Zymurgy is the art of brewing, wine-making or distilling.

100. Zephyr A zephyr is a pleasant, light breeze that you'd welcome on a hot summer day. "A passing zephyr rustled through the treetops." Ah! Poetic!

Brought to you by,
https://wordcounter.net/blog/2016/12/19/102744_words-you-should-know.html

How to Say Hello & Goodbye in Spanish, French, and 20+ Languages

Spanish: Buenos dias!/Adios!

You might already know these phrases from your favorite movies or music. Be warned that different Spanish-speaking countries might have variations on their greetings, though most everyone will be willing to give you a 'hola' in return.

French: Bonjour!/Au revoir!

The French love wishing you a "good day." Along with it sounding particularly romantic, 'au revoir' is quite touching—it literally translates into "until I see you again."

Italian: Ciao!/Ciao!

The Italians make it easy. While you can get more technical if you would like (buongiorno/arrivederci), a simple greeting suits the usually-friendly Italian people.

German: Hallo!/ Auf Wiedershen!

As with much of the German language, it might take some practice to get all of those syllables down. Once you've got it, though, locals will appreciate the effort you're making to connect.

Dutch: Hallo!/ Tot ziens!
Thankfully, 'hello' is quite easy in a number of different languages. It's always saying goodbye that ends up being the most difficult!

Japanese: Kon' nichiwa!/Sayonara !
Japanese isn't known for being the easiest language to learn, but just knowing how to greet someone can bridge some cultural barriers. Everyone likes to know that you've taken the time to learn about a certain language.

Greek: Geia!/Anito!
Few countries are friendlier than Greece, and when you can say a few things in the Greek language, you're sure to get plenty of smiles (and maybe even a free pastry or coffee).

Korean: Annyeong!/Jalga!
In a bustling city like Seoul, it's good to know a few words so you can get around. This greeting can be a great way to introduce yourself in order to get some directions or to make a new friend.

Hindi: Hailo!/Alavida!
We can see the roots of our Indo-European language of English in this greeting. (Looks familiar to the German 'hallo,' right?) It makes it slightly easier to communicate when you feel overwhelmed by India and its history.

Arabic: Ahlan!/Ma' a as-salaama!
Before you say this to the opposite gender in an Arabic-speaking country, remember that it is inappropriate in a public setting (unless otherwise expressed). And always shake hands with your right one!

Croatian: Pozdravite!/Pozdravite!

Thankfully, you only have to remember one word when you plan to begin and end a conversation in Croatia. This can be especially helpful since the Croatian language isn't known for being the easiest one to learn.

Mandarin: Nǐ hǎo!/Zàijiàn!
Before you share this greeting on your next trip to China, remember that there are two types of the Chinese language. You'll want to know which areas are Mandarin-speaking and which speak Cantonese.

Danish: Hej!/Farvel!
The Danes are known for their interesting sense of humor and often perfect English. However, you're more likely to get a friendly reaction if you try and say 'hello' like the locals.

Hungarian: Helló!/Viszlát!
A good way to make a new friend in Hungary? Just say 'hello'! Well, with a little bit of an inflection. A farewell might be a bit harder to pronounce, but it's often

welcome after being served up a steaming cup of goulash.

Indonesian: Halo!/Selamat tinggal!
Throw out these phrases on your next trip to Bali and impress your friends. Who knew that saying goodbye could be such a mouthful? (But the locals will be grateful that you tried.)

Cantonese: Néih hóu!/Joigin!
Once you've identified which Chinese language you want to use, make sure to give it a try. No one is expecting that you will get it perfect, and many are happy to just see you try and engage with their culture.

Russian: Privet!/Poka!
This farewell is a little bit easier than what you will hear in pop culture ('dasvidaniya' can be quite difficult depending on how well you know Russian). Regardless, it can be a good way to speak with a friend over a glass of strong vodka.

Norwegian: Hei!/Hade!
It might be easy to get these two greetings confused, but many Norwegians have almost perfect English and can help you with their language. It can be a great way to introduce yourself to some of the locals (and maybe get a free language lesson).

Khmer: Suostei!/Lea!
When you are headed to Angkor Wat on your Cambodian journey, feel free to throw out some Khmer phrases. The locals are some of the friendliest people on the planet and will be grateful that you tried to make a new acquaintance.

Finnish: Hei!/ Näkemiin!
When heading up north, you only need to know 'hei' in order to greet someone new. It's not only easy to remember, but everyone in Scandinavian countries will understand what you are saying.

Maltese: Bonjour!/Addiju!

The tiny island country of Malta has been a crossroads of history and culture for hundreds of years. Likewise, you'll find bits of French and Italian in their language. However, there are parts that are all their own too.

Swahili: Hello!/Kwaheri!

Over 5 million people speak Swahili as a native language in Africa, and even more speak it as a second language (135 million). English speakers won't have a hard time saying 'hello'—it's the same in both languages!

Icelandic: Halló!/Bless!

As one of the most difficult languages in the world to learn, it's refreshing to know that greetings aren't much of a stretch. Either way, you should have no issues getting around Iceland—everyone speaks perfect English (though it doesn't mean locals won't appreciate the gesture).

Bulgarian: Zdravei !/Dovizhdane !

Bulgarian isn't an easy language to read—or to speak. But as it becomes a more popular tourist destination, it never hurts to be able to let the local people know that you're interested in their culture and history.
Brought to you by
https://www.rypeapp.com/blog/how-to-say-hello-goodbye-in-spanish-french-and-more/

Common rules of 21st Century Etiquette

You'll notice a common denominator in all of them: Think about other people's feelings first because it's not all about maximizing your personal convenience.

1. Texting "Hey, I'm running 20 minutes late" is not as acceptable as making the effort to be on time.

2. If you can't attend an event that you're formally invited to, don't think that not RSVPing is the same as declining. And don't RSVP at the last minute for an event that involves real planning by the host.

3. Show some decency around the office refrigerator: If you didn't put the food in, don't eat it. And take your leftovers home or throw them out before they morph into some radioactive nightmare.

4. Don't bellow on your cell phone. Just because you can't hear the other person well doesn't mean the other person can't hear you well.

5. Turn off the phone at a dinner party, and be in the moment. You're annoying at least one person who thinks you have no social skills. At bare minimum, turn off the ringer so you can text and conspire in relative stealth.

6. Remember that if you feel a need to respond immediately to every incoming text, you'll lose more in the eyes of the person who's in front of you than you'll gain from the unseen people who are benefiting from your efficiency.

7. When you get to the front of the line at Starbucks , don't tell the barista to wait while you wrap up your phone discussion. The barista hates you, and so does everyone behind you. They are hoping the barista spits in your latte.

8. If you come late to an exercise class, don't think you're entitled to barge your way to your favorite spot in the front.   And don't block others from weight racks or other equipment—just step back three feet and make everyone happy.

9. Keep personal conversations and arguments off social networking sites. The dramatic airing of grievances is best done through SMS .

10. Moderate your use of cameras and video at events. Enjoy your time with colleagues, friends and family in the present and preserve only a memento for the future, rather than recording the entire thing to "relive" later in some "free" time that you'll never actually have.

11. Remember how easily e-gossip can be forwarded along to the wrong person.

12. Just because you're wearing headphones doesn't mean you can tune out from social courtesies. For example, if you accidentally cross someone's personal space, apologize graciously.

13. Don't lend someone a book or item unless they specifically ask for it. They're probably too busy to ever get around to it. They'll feel guilty about that, and you'll be annoyed that they didn't appreciate it or even get around to returning it.

14. Don't RSVP for an event, then not show. Now you're not just being rude, but you're costing the host money, and you've probably kept a lonely soul from being invited as a backup.

15. Don't be the first or second person to talk on your cell phone in a public space (like a bus or train). If everyone's doing it, you're allowed some slack here.

16. Don't show up at a party empty-handed, unless you've been instructed to -- and sometimes not even then. Bring wine or dessert or a plant.

17. Use your turn signal at least 50% more than you use your middle finger.

18. Don't make your dietary requirements everyone else's dilemma. As one friend reminds me, "People who can eat dairy don't just keep coconut oil-based butter around."

19. If your children are invited to a friend's house to play, they (and you) should also feel invited to help with the cleanup.

20. Don't break up with someone by text. And don't announce a death in the family by text. There are still times when phones or face-to-face are the best way to go.

21. Don't take photos for posting on the People of Walmart page.

22. Don't discuss sensitive personal issues on Facebook, especially if you've friended coworkers.

23. Your dog is cute, but he or she doesn't have a pass to go anywhere.

24. Double-check that your headphones are plugged-in before streaming your favorite Spotify station.

25. Don't say, "I'm having a party. Bring your own food and drink." That's not a party.

26. If you've been invited to an event, be reluctant to ask for an upper ceiling on how many friends and relatives you can bring.

27. And finally, all the classics still apply. One working mother offers a quick review here:

Chew with your mouth closed; don't talk with food in your mouth; keep your elbows off of the table while eating; wash your hands after going to the restroom. My children know better—so why do I see adults exhibiting such poor behavior? If you bump into someone, say excuse me. Don't reach across someone's face. Don't board a plane when they're loading group A and you are in group D. Don't stay behind the crosswalk when you are making a left turn and thus prevent anyone else behind you from turning. Don't let your kids act like wild monkeys in a restaurant. Don't touch someone's belly when she's pregnant--or even when she isn't. Don't leave cupboard doors and drawers open—someone can get hurt. And don't pull up to the exit gate in a parking lot without your ticket handy."

Remember the basic success principle, underlying all manners: Think about other people's feelings first… because, it's still not all about you.

Brought to you by…

https://www.forbes.com/sites/robasghar/2014/04/22/27-etiquette-rules-for-our-times/?sh=633446f53dc3

Here's 10 excerpts from Selassie's speeches.

Haile Selassie I, original name Tafari Makonnen, (born July 23, 1892, near Harer, Ethiopia—died August 27, 1975, Addis Ababa), emperor of Ethiopia from 1930 to 1974 who sought to modernize his country and who steered it into the mainstream of post-World War II African politics.
Born: July 23, 1892

Died: August 27, 1975

Kingdom: Ethiopia

Founded: Organisation of African Unity

1. "Today, we look to the future calmly, confidently, and courageously. We look to the vision of an Africa not merely free but united. In facing this new challenge, we can take comfort and encouragement from the lessons of the past. We know that there are differences among us. Africans enjoy different cultures,

distinctive values, special attributes. But we also know that unity can be and has been attained among men of the most disparate origins, that differences of race, of religion, of culture, of tradition, are no insuperable obstacle to the coming together of peoples. History teaches us that unity is strength". —Words of H.I.M. Emperor Haile Selassie in Addis Ababa May 25, 1963, Speech, "Towards African Unity"

On leadership

2. "Leadership does not mean domination. The world is always well supplied with people who wish to rule and dominate others. The true leader is a different sort; he seeks effective activity which has a truly beneficient purpose. He inspires others to follow in his wake, and holding aloft the torch of wisdom, leads the way for society to realize its genuinely great aspirations". —Speech on Leadership in Speeches Delivered on Various Occasions.

On science and religion

3. "The progress of science can be said to be harmful to religion only in so far as it is used for evil aims and not because it claims a priority over religion in its revelation to man. It is important that spiritual advancement must keep pace with material advancement". — Interview in The Voice of Ethiopia (5 April 1948).

Views on education

4. "Education is a means of sharpening the mind of man both spiritually and intellectually. It is a two-edged sword that can be used either for the progress of mankind or for its destruction. That is why it has been Our constant desire and endeavor to develop our education for the benefit of mankind".

5. "Throughout history, it has been the inaction of those who could have acted, the indifference of those who should have known better, the silence of the voice of justice when it mattered most, that has made it possible for evil to triumph". — Cited as from an address in Addis Ababa (1963).

On the question of racial discrimination

6. "That until the philosophy which holds one race superior and another inferior is finally and permanently discredited and abandoned; That until there are no longer first-class and second-class citizens of any nation; That until the color of a man's skin is of no more significance than the color of his eyes; That until the basic human rights are equally guaranteed to all without regard to race; That until that day, the dream of lasting peace and world citizenship and the rule of international morality will remain but a fleeting illusion, to be pursued but never attained".

7. "And until the ignoble and unhappy regimes that hold our brothers in Angola, in Mozambique and in South Africa in subhuman bondage have been toppled and destroyed; Until bigotry and prejudice and malicious and inhuman self-interest have been replaced by understanding and tolerance and good-will; Until all Africans stand and speak as free beings, equal in the eyes of

all men, as they are in the eyes of Heaven;
Until that day, the African continent will
not know peace. We Africans will fight,
if necessary, and we know that we shall
win, as we are confident in the victory of
good over evil". – Haile Selassie I.

8. "Men on other parts of this earth
occupied themselves with their own
concerns and, in their conceit, proclaimed
that the world began and ended at their
horizons. All unknown to them, Africa
developed in its own pattern, growing in
its own life and, in the nineteenth century,
finally re-emerged into the world's
consciousness".

On colonialism, nuclear testing

9. "We demand an end to colonialism
because domination of one people by
another is wrong. We demand an end to
nuclear testing and the arms race because
these activities, which pose such dreadful
threats to man's existence, and waste and
squander humanity's material heritage,
are wrong. We demand an end to racial
segregation as an affront to man's dignity

which is wrong. We act in these matters in the right, as a matter of high principle. We act out of the integrity and conviction of our most deep-founded beliefs".
—Speech, "Towards African Unity" 1963.

10. "It is no less important that we know whence we came. An awareness of our past is essential to the establishment of our personality and our identity as Africans". —Speech, "Towards African Unity"Brought to you byhttps://thisisafrica.me/politics-and-soci ety/remembering-emperor-haile-selassie-10-profound-quotes/

Body Language 101

*Study the Eyes. … are they shifty

*Gaze at the Face – skin care, expressions, movements

*Touching Mouth or Smiling- timing

*Pay attention to proximity- be aware of your surroundings

*See if the other person is mirroring you-are they mocking your personality to fit

*Observe the head movement-the mouth may say yes, but the head may say no…all must be in tandem

**Look at the other person's feet- if they are planted toward you you have a mostly civil situation, but if one foot is always in the opposite direction…watch out

*Watch for hand signals-watch for steady or figgidy hands and jerky movements

*Examine the position of the arms-remember crossed arms for someone on defense- open chest for one that has nothing to hide

Now!
Do you feel like
a
KING?